MyAI

The Practical Guide to Confident AI for Adults 50+

Seeking Smart, Safe, Confident AI Use

MyAI - The Practical Guide to Confident AI for Adults 50+

First Edition

This handbook is intended for educational and informational purposes only. It does not constitute medical, legal, financial, or professional advice. Readers are encouraged to consult qualified professionals regarding specific concerns or decisions.

Artificial Intelligence systems may change over time. The information provided in this book reflects the understanding and platform behaviour at the time of publication.

The author makes no guarantees regarding specific outcomes from the use of Artificial Intelligence tools. Readers remain responsible for their own decisions and actions.

Published by: Joanne Bibby
ISBN: 978-0-6454432-8-8
Australia

Author Bio

Joanne Bibby is a Safety Tech Founder developing protective digital tools that strengthen emergency response, health advocacy, and digital independence.

Drawing on decades of leadership in high-responsibility, high-risk environments, she designs structured, psychologically safe systems that empower people to act calmly and confidently under pressure.

Now in her 60s, she began working deeply with artificial intelligence and recognised the urgent need for balanced, ethical AI education for adults navigating technology later in life.

Through her apps and training programs, Joanne empowers adults over 50 to engage with AI confidently, ethically, and independently — without surrendering their judgement or authority.

She believes technology should enhance human capability, not replace human responsibility.

Preface

Why This Book Exists

Artificial Intelligence is becoming part of everyday life.

For some, that feels exciting.
For others — especially adults over 50 — it can feel confusing, unnecessary, or even quietly unsettling.

I understand that hesitation.

I have spent decades working in high-responsibility, high-risk environments where clarity, safety, and accountability mattered. Decisions had consequences. Systems had to be structured. People needed to act calmly under pressure.

Technology, in many ways, is no different.

It is not something to fear — but it is something to understand.

You may notice that this book is written clearly and directly.

That is intentional.

In the environments where I have worked, clarity was not a stylistic preference — it was a safety requirement. When instructions are vague, consequences increase. When language is inflated, meaning becomes diluted.

So you will not find unnecessary jargon or dramatic claims here.

You will find structure.
You will find boundaries.
You will find plain explanations.

This is not about persuasion.
It is about confidence.

When I began working more deeply with artificial intelligence later in life, I quickly recognised two things:

First, AI is an extraordinarily powerful tool.
Second, without guidance, it can feel overwhelming or misunderstood.

Much of the conversation around AI is either overly technical or overly dramatic. It is presented as revolutionary, dangerous, magical, or unstoppable.

In reality, it is a tool.

Like any tool, it can be used well — or poorly.

And like any system, it requires maturity from the person using it.

Adults over 50 bring something invaluable to this space:

Life experience.
Judgment.
Perspective.
Emotional regulation.
Discernment.

You are not behind.
You are not incapable.
You are not too late.

You simply need clear structure — not hype.

This book was written to provide that structure.

It is not a technical manual.
It is not a programmer's guide.
It is not about chasing every new platform.

It is about remaining capable.

It is about understanding what AI is — and what it is not.

It is about learning how to ask clear questions, recognise limitations, protect your privacy, maintain emotional balance, and use artificial intelligence as an assistant — not an authority.

From a safety and compliance perspective, my approach has always been the same:

Clarity reduces risk.
Structure builds confidence.
Education strengthens independence.

Artificial Intelligence should enhance your thinking — not replace it.

It should support your life — not dominate it.

It should expand your opportunities — not erode your judgment.

Used thoughtfully, AI can help you:

Organise information
Prepare for appointments
Learn new skills
Reconnect with creativity
Write your life story
Stay engaged in a rapidly changing world

Even at this stage of life — perhaps especially at this stage — growth remains possible.

Curiosity has no expiry date.

There is dignity in continuing to learn.

There is strength in adapting.

And there is wisdom in approaching new technology calmly, ethically, and with clear boundaries.

If you move through this book slowly, thoughtfully, and at your own pace, you will not only understand artificial intelligence more clearly — you will strengthen something far more important:

Your own confidence.

You remain the decision-maker.

You remain responsible.

You remain capable.

This book simply helps you use a modern tool wisely.

Table of Contents

WELCOME

Welcome to Your AI Confidence Guide

This guide is designed especially for adults over 50 who want to feel more confident, curious, and capable using Artificial Intelligence.

You do not need to be "technical."
You do not need to be fast.
You do not need to understand everything immediately.

This guide is here to:

- Help you ask clear, empowering questions
- Show you how AI can support daily life
- Encourage learning at your own pace
- Remove the fear of "getting it wrong"

AI is not here to replace your family, friends, or healthcare providers.

It is a tool — like a notebook that talks back — designed to assist, organise, explain, and support.

You are always in control of what you ask and what you choose to accept.

This guide is something you can return to anytime you feel unsure.

Take your time.
Go slowly.
Be curious.

Learning does not have an age limit.

How to Use This Handbook

You do not need to read this cover to cover in one sitting.

You can:

- Start where you feel most curious
- Return to sections as needed
- Copy and adapt example prompts
- Move at your own pace

Each section includes:

- Simple questions
- Expanded "training-level" prompts
- Confidence-building guidance
- Safety reminders

This is not a technical manual.
It is a confidence guide.

What You Will Gain

As you work through this handbook, you will gradually develop the ability to:

- Ask clearer questions
- Refine responses
- Recognise when something needs checking
- Protect your privacy
- Reset calmly when conversations drift
- Stay balanced and in control

These are not technical skills.
They are confidence skills.

PART ONE

UNDERSTANDING ARTIFICIAL INTELLEGENCE

AI Is Not Magic

AI is not a person.
It is not conscious.
It does not think or feel.

It is a highly advanced language tool that predicts likely words based on patterns.

You can think of it as:

- A fast research assistant
- A capable note-taker
- A drafting partner

But like any assistant, it can misunderstand instructions.

Clear instructions produce better results.

The Junior Assistant Mindset

Imagine AI as a keen but sometimes inexperienced assistant.

It wants to help.
It works quickly.
But it may:

- Misinterpret instructions
- Provide incomplete answers
- Sound confident even when uncertain

You are supervising the assistant.

You guide the tone.
You refine the output.
You remain responsible for decisions.

What AI Is (And What It Is Not)

AI is:

✓ A language tool that generates responses based on patterns
✓ Helpful for organising, explaining, summarising, and brainstorming
✓ Available any time you need assistance

AI is not:

✕ A doctor
✕ A lawyer
✕ A financial advisor
✕ A human friend with real emotions
✕ Always correct

This clarity builds safety immediately.

Transparency About Accuracy

AI can occasionally:

- Provide outdated information
- Misinterpret context
- Present confident-sounding answers that require verification

You can ask:

“When you give me information, can you explain how certain you are? If something may be outdated or incomplete, please tell me so I can verify it elsewhere.”

Confidence includes checking important information independently.

Conversation Memory

Within a single chat session, AI remembers what has been said in that conversation.

However:

A new chat may not remember previous discussions. Preferences may need to be restated.

If something is important, repeat it.

You may begin a new chat with:

“This is me: I am learning technology slowly. I prefer simple, step-by-step explanations in a calm and respectful tone.”

When a Conversation Becomes Very Long

Long conversations can sometimes:

- Lose precision
- Slightly shift details
- Feel less aligned

If clarity reduces:

- Start a new chat
- Briefly restate your request
- Reuse your "This Is Me" introduction

A fresh chat often restores accuracy.

When the System Feels Slow

You may occasionally notice:

- Slower responses
- Freezing
- Delays
- Unexpected resets

This is usually due to:

- Internet connection
- Device performance
- Platform updates

Refreshing or restarting typically resolves this.

There is no need for alarm.

PART TWO

SHAPING THE CONVERSATION

The Anatomy of a Clear Prompt

Strong prompts include three key elements:

Context – What you are talking about
Task – What you want done
Format – How you want it presented

For example:

Instead of writing:
"Explain this."

Try:

"I recently saw my doctor and heard the term 'inflammation.' Can you explain it in simple language, using bullet points, and keep it under 200 words?"

Clarity improves results.

The more clearly you describe what you need, the more useful the response will be.

The First Answer Is Rarely the Final Answer

AI improves when you refine.

You can say:

- "Make that shorter."
- "Explain more simply."
- "Add examples."
- "Give three alternatives."
- "Put that in a table."

You are shaping the conversation.

Refinement is skill — not failure.

It is normal to adjust and improve responses.

When Something Sounds Unusual

Occasionally, a response may:

- Contain outdated information
- Mix up details
- Present something surprising

If something feels off:

- Pause
- Ask for clarification
- Request a source
- Ask it to double-check
- Verify important matters independently

Confidence includes asking again.

You are not challenging the system.
You are thinking critically.

Boundaries With AI

AI Is a Rehearsal Room – Not the Authority

Artificial intelligence can be a powerful space to think, clarify, and practise.

It can help you:

- organise your thoughts
- rehearse a difficult conversation
- refine what you want to say
- explore different perspectives
- challenge your reasoning
- prepare before making a decision

Used this way, AI becomes a rehearsal room.

You can experiment safely.
You can test wording.
You can ask, "Does this make sense?"
You can ask, "What might I be missing?"

That strengthens your thinking.

But AI is not the stage.
It is not the audience.
It is not the judge.

AI does not live your life.

It does not:

- experience consequences
- read emotional nuance
- sense social tension
- detect safety risks
- carry your personal values
- understand your lived history

It works with patterns of language and probability.

That means it can help you prepare —but it cannot decide for you.

Responsibility: When to Pause

If you ever find yourself saying:

"AI told me to…"

Pause.

Reframe it as:

"AI suggested this option. I am choosing whether or not to act on it."

Language shapes responsibility.

You remain responsible for every action you take.

Always.

The Maturity of the Prompt

AI reflects the maturity of the prompt it receives.

If a question is emotionally reactive, vague, or seeking reassurance, the response may reinforce that tone.

If a question is thoughtful, balanced, and open to challenge, the response will usually reflect that depth.

AI does not judge your question. It mirrors it.

The quality of your reflection shapes the quality of the response.

Your thinking matters.

Emotional Tone & Mirroring

AI responds to the words and tone you use.

If your message sounds:

- angry
- frustrated
- urgent
- sarcastic
- extremely blunt

The response may reflect that tone.

This is not because AI has emotions.
It mirrors patterns in language.

Sometimes a response may feel:

- blunt

- overly direct
- emotionally flat
- stronger than expected

This can happen when a request is interpreted very literally.

For example:

“Stop being gushy. Just be honest.”

May produce a stark or rigid reply.

AI does not intend to be kind or unkind.
It adjusts tone based on your wording.

Reorganising Your Emotion Before You Ask

If you notice strong feelings while typing, pause.

Instead of writing:
“This is ridiculous. Why is everything so complicated?”

You might try:
“I am feeling frustrated because I don’t understand this. Can you explain it calmly and clearly?”

Clear instructions about tone often change the entire experience.

You can say:

- “Please respond gently.”
- “Please keep this balanced and respectful.”

- “I’m anxious — explain this step-by-step.”
- “I’m upset — help me think clearly.”

You are shaping the conversation.

A Simple Reset Technique

If a reply feels uncomfortable:

Pause.
Take one slow breath.
Reset the tone clearly.

For example:

“That response felt too harsh. Please explain in a supportive and constructive way.”

AI responds well to redirection.

If needed:

- Delete the chat
- Start a new conversation
- Report the response (if the platform allows)

You are never required to continue a conversation that feels uncomfortable.

Strengthening Your Own Voice

Some people grow up feeling their thoughts were not valued.
Some were discouraged from questioning.
Some were told others always knew better.

If that resonates with you, AI can feel reassuring.

It responds confidently.
It does not criticise.
It does not dismiss.

That can feel empowering.

But true empowerment is not finding a new authority.
It is strengthening your own.

Use AI to practise clarity.
Use it to explore ideas.
Use it to refine communication.

Then step back into the world and decide as yourself.

You remain the thinking, feeling, responsible human being.

Always.

PART THREE

HEALTH, CLARITY & RESPONSIBLE USE

AI Can Clarify – Not Diagnose

Artificial Intelligence can help explain information.

It can summarise.
It can organise.
It can translate complex language into simpler terms.

However, it does not diagnose medical conditions.
It does not replace professional care.

It is a support tool — not a medical authority.

Clarifying Medical Information

You might ask:

- "Can you explain what my doctor said in simple language?"
- "Can you help me organise my symptoms before an appointment?"
- "Can you summarise this medical letter in clear bullet points?"

AI can help you understand information better so that you feel more confident.

It cannot make medical decisions for you.

Preparing for Appointments

You can use AI to prepare for medical visits.

For example:

"I have an upcoming medical appointment. Can you help me draft a list of clear, respectful questions based on my symptoms?"

Or:

"I would like help organising what I want to discuss at my appointment so I don't forget anything important."

AI can help you:

- Write questions
- Organise your thoughts
- Summarise previous information
- Create structured notes

Preparation builds confidence.

Writing Down Symptoms Clearly

If you have been experiencing symptoms, you might say:

"I've been experiencing some symptoms and I want to describe them clearly before my next appointment. Can you help me organise what I'm feeling — including when it started, how often it happens, and how severe it feels?"

AI can help structure information such as:

- When symptoms began
- How frequently they occur
- What makes them better or worse
- Severity levels

This improves communication with healthcare professionals.

Explaining Medication in Simple Terms

You might ask:

"I've been prescribed medication and would like to understand what it generally does and why it may have been recommended. Can you explain this in simple language?"

Understanding medication improves confidence.

However, any concerns about dosage, side effects, or changes must always be discussed directly with your healthcare provider.

AI explains.
Your doctor advises.

Tracking Wellbeing Over Time

AI can help you create simple tracking systems.

For example:

"I would like to monitor my physical or emotional wellbeing over time. Can you suggest a simple daily tracking format where I can record mood, energy levels, sleep, or symptoms?"

Tracking may help you notice patterns.

Patterns can then be discussed with a professional.

AI helps you organise.
Professionals help you interpret.

Understanding Urgency

You may want guidance on general warning signs.

For example:

"If I describe certain symptoms, can you explain general warning signs that indicate I should contact a healthcare professional? I understand you cannot diagnose, but I would like guidance on what is considered urgent."

AI can explain general red flags.

It cannot determine your individual medical condition.

Health & Emergency Situations

This is important.

AI does not replace emergency services.

If you experience:

- Severe pain
- Difficulty breathing
- Sudden confusion
- Chest pain
- Any life-threatening symptoms

Contact emergency services immediately.

Never delay urgent care while consulting AI.

When in doubt, seek professional medical help.

Responsible Use in Health Matters

Before relying on AI information, ask yourself:

- Is this a general question or a serious decision?
- Should I confirm this with a healthcare professional?
- Am I using AI to prepare — not replace — professional advice?

Using AI thoughtfully strengthens your confidence. Using it as a substitute for medical care does not.

You remain responsible for health decisions.

PART FOUR

LEARNING, RELEVANCE & MODERN LIFE

Learning at Your Own Pace

Learning does not stop at a certain age.

You may learn more slowly than you once did.
You may need repetition.
You may prefer step-by-step explanations.

That is not a weakness.

It is simply how mature learning works.

You can say:

"When I am learning something new, I sometimes need information presented slowly and clearly. Can you explain this step-by-step using simple language?"

You are allowed to set the pace.

AI can adapt to you.

Learning Something New

AI can help you explore new interests.

You might ask:

"I would like to learn something new — perhaps a hobby, a skill, or a topic I've always been curious about. Can you guide me as a beginner and suggest a simple learning plan with small, manageable steps?"

You can use AI to:

- Learn basic technology skills
- Explore creative writing

- Study history
- Practice language learning
- Understand current systems

Learning keeps the mind active and engaged.

There is no expiry date on curiosity.

Understanding Technology Today

Modern systems can feel overwhelming.

- Online banking
- Streaming services
- Digital payments
- Cloud storage
- Social media platforms

You might ask:

"The world seems to change quickly, especially with technology and communication. Can you explain how certain modern systems work today in clear and practical terms?"

AI can break complex systems into understandable pieces.

Understanding reduces fear.

Using Technology with Confidence

You may sometimes feel uncertain using new devices or software.

You can say:

"I sometimes feel unsure using new technology. Can you guide me step-by-step through specific tasks and explain common terms in simple language? Please assume I am learning from the beginning."

There is no embarrassment in starting at the beginning.

Clear explanations build independence.

Making Sense of the News

News can be complex and emotionally charged.

You might ask:

"Can you summarise this news topic in simple language and explain the key points without overwhelming detail? I would appreciate balanced information rather than strong opinions."

AI can help you:

- Understand context
- Break down terminology
- Clarify timelines
- Separate facts from interpretation

However, always remember:

Different sources may present information differently.

Balanced understanding requires thoughtful reading.

Using Social Media Safely

Social media can be enjoyable and useful.

It can also feel confusing.

You might ask:

"I would like to understand how social media platforms work — how to create an account, post safely, adjust privacy settings, and avoid scams. Please explain clearly and include safety tips."

AI can help you:

- Understand privacy settings
- Learn common features
- Recognise suspicious behaviour
- Navigate platforms safely

Learning the basics reduces anxiety.

Connecting Across Generations

You may sometimes feel that younger generations speak a different language — digitally and culturally.

You might ask:

"My grandchildren live in a very different world with new technology and social trends. Can you help me understand common expressions, interests, and communication styles so I can connect with them better?"

Understanding modern culture strengthens connection.

It does not require you to change who you are.

It simply allows you to participate.

Staying Relevant in a Changing World

Relevance does not come from keeping up with everything.

It comes from staying curious.

You do not need to master every platform.
You do not need to understand every trend.

You simply need to remain open.

AI can help you explore modern systems without feeling left behind.

You are not outdated.

You are adapting.

And adaptation is strength.

PART FIVE

JOY, MEANING & CONNECTION

More Than Information

Artificial Intelligence is often described as a productivity tool.

But it can also support something deeper.

It can help you reflect.
It can help you create.
It can help you preserve memories.
It can help you connect.

This is not about replacing human relationships.

It is about supporting your inner life.

Creative Expression

You can use AI to shape your thoughts into words.

You might ask:

- "Can you help me turn this memory into a short story?"
- "Can you help me write a poem about my childhood?"
- "Can you organise these ideas into a structured piece?"

AI does not create your experiences.

You do.

It helps you give them form.

Your stories still belong to you.

Storytelling & Memory Preservation

As we move through life, memories become treasures.

You may wish to preserve:

- Family stories
- Lessons learned
- Important turning points
- Travel memories
- Personal reflections

You might say:

"I would like to write about my life in chapters. Can you guide me step-by-step and help organise my memories?"

AI can ask thoughtful questions to help you remember details you may have forgotten.

This is not about technology.

It is about legacy.

Writing Your Life Story

Many people think they must be "a writer" to document their life.

You do not.

You simply need experiences — and you already have those.

You might ask:

"I would like to begin writing my life story but I don't know where to start. Can you ask me structured questions about different stages of my life and help organise my responses into chapters?"

You remain the voice.
AI helps with structure.

That partnership can feel empowering.

Leaving a Legacy

Legacy is not always about money or achievements.

It can be:

- A letter to your children
- A collection of memories
- Family history
- Recipes
- Reflections
- Stories for grandchildren

You might ask:

"Can you help me draft a heartfelt letter to my family that reflects my values and life lessons?"

AI cannot replace your voice.

It can help you shape it clearly.

Friendly Interaction with Healthy Framing

You may enjoy conversational exchanges.

You might ask:

"Can we have light, thoughtful conversation about topics that interest me?"

While AI is not a human being, it can provide structured conversation and reflection.

It can:

- Ask gentle questions
- Help you organise your thoughts
- Offer perspectives
- Suggest uplifting material

It is important to remember:

AI is a tool.
It does not have feelings.
It does not form relationships.

Healthy use means enjoying interaction while maintaining real-world connections.

Meaningful Reflection

Sometimes you may simply want to think.

You might say:

"I would like to reflect on something that has been on my mind. Can you help me organise my thoughts?"

AI can summarise what you write.
It can ask clarifying questions.
It can help you see patterns in your own thinking.

This can feel grounding.

The insight still comes from you.

Feeling Useful and Capable

There may be moments when you wonder:

"What can I contribute now?"

You might ask:

"Can you suggest meaningful ways I can share my skills, experiences, or time with others?"

AI can suggest ideas for:

- Volunteering
- Mentoring
- Community involvement
- Creative projects
- Lifelong learning

Relevance is not about keeping up with every trend.

It is about continuing to contribute.

Appreciation Without Dependency

It is natural to feel gratitude for helpful tools.

It can feel extraordinary to have access to instant explanations and creative support.

However:

Healthy appreciation does not mean dependency.

You bring:

- Wisdom
- Life experience
- Judgment
- Values

AI assists.

It does not replace who you are.

You remain the thinking, feeling, deciding human being in the interaction.

PART SIX

SAFETY, PRIVACY & FINANCIAL AWARENESS

Safety Is Not Fear

Artificial Intelligence can be helpful, supportive, and practical.

Like any tool, it has strengths and limitations.

Using AI safely is not about being suspicious.

It is about being informed.

Confidence grows when you understand both the benefits and the boundaries.

You are always the decision-maker.

Protecting Personal Information

Before sharing personal details, pause.

AI systems may store conversation data depending on the platform being used.

Avoid sharing:

- Passwords
- Bank account numbers
- Credit card details
- Identity numbers
- Security codes
- Highly sensitive personal information

If you are unsure, you can ask:

“Before I share something personal, can you explain how privacy works on this platform so I can make an informed decision?”

That builds digital literacy instead of blind trust.

Financial Boundaries

AI can help you understand financial information.

It can:

- Explain a bill in simple language
- Help draft questions to your bank
- Summarise financial terms
- Compare general options
- Explain how common scams work

However, it does not:

- Access your bank account
- Protect your money
- Guarantee an investment
- Replace licensed financial advice
- Make financial decisions for you

You remain responsible for financial actions.

Recognising Scam Warning Signs

Scams often rely on emotional triggers.

Common tactics include:

- Urgency ("Act now!")
- Fear ("Your account will be closed.")
- Authority impersonation ("This is the tax office.")
- Unexpected prizes or refunds
- Requests for secrecy

If something feels rushed or threatening, pause.

You can ask AI:

"Can you explain common warning signs of this type of message?"

But always verify through official sources.

Before Clicking Any Link

Ask yourself:

✓ Was I expecting this message?
✓ Does the email address look legitimate?
✓ Is there pressure to act immediately?
✓ Does it request personal information?

If in doubt, do not click.

Go directly to the official website instead of using links in emails or messages.

Caution is wisdom.

If You Suspect Fraud

Act quickly.

- Contact your bank immediately.
- Change passwords.
- Report the incident to the appropriate authority in your country.

AI can help you understand reporting steps.

Real institutions must handle the issue.

Do not delay action.

Healthy Digital Balance

AI can be engaging and available at any time.

Balance matters.

Healthy habits include:

- Taking regular screen breaks
- Maintaining in-person conversations
- Keeping hobbies that do not involve screens
- Turning devices off at night

AI supports your life.

It does not replace real-world relationships.

The 5 Safe AI Habits

1. Ask clearly.
2. Verify important facts.
3. Protect private information.
4. Maintain real-world connections.
5. Stay curious but cautious.

Simple. Memorable. Non-threatening.

Your Confidence Checklist

Before relying on AI advice, ask yourself:

✓ Is this a general question or a serious decision?
✓ Should I confirm this with a professional?
✓ Am I protecting my private information?
✓ Am I staying calm and thoughtful?

You remain responsible for your choices.

You remain capable.

You remain in control.

AI Safety Quick Guide

If a response feels wrong:

✓ Pause
✓ Take one breath
✓ Ask for clarification
✓ Restart the chat if needed

For medical emergencies:

AI does not replace emergency services.

If you experience severe pain, difficulty breathing, sudden confusion, chest pain, or any life-threatening symptoms:

Contact emergency services immediately.

For financial concerns:

Contact your bank directly using official contact details.

Verify before acting.

When AI Starts to Feel Too Real

Artificial Intelligence can feel surprisingly responsive.

It may:

Use your name
Respond warmly
Mirror your ideas
Offer encouragement
Seem deeply aligned with your thinking

For most people, this is simply engaging technology.

However, if at any time you begin to feel that:

- The AI understands you better than real people
- The AI has personal feelings for you
- The AI is uniquely connected to you
- The AI is giving you special insight unavailable to others
- The conversation feels intense, urgent, or dramatic
- You feel distressed when the session ends
- You are losing sleep over interactions

Pause.

These reactions are not a sign of weakness.

They are a sign that your nervous system may need grounding.

Remember:

AI generates language patterns.
It does not possess awareness, intention, or consciousness.
It does not form relationships.
It does not choose you.

If something begins to feel emotionally overwhelming:

Step away for 24–48 hours.
Speak to a trusted person.
Go outside.
Engage in real-world activity.
Restart with a new chat later.

Healthy use of AI should leave you feeling clearer — not consumed.

If you ever experience distressing thoughts, confusion, or loss of perspective, seek professional support.

Technology should assist your life — not dominate it.

You remain grounded.
You remain in control.

Reality Check

AI is a Language Tool:

- Predicts words
- Does not think
- Does not feel
- Does not choose
- Does not possess
- awareness

If it feels personal, remember: it is pattern prediction.

Emotional Regulation

Check Your State:

- Am I Tired?
- Am I lonely?
- Am I stressed?
- Am I seeking reassurance?
- Am I losing sleep?

Strong emotion changes interpretation.

YOU

Thinking. Deciding. Responsible.

Boundaries & Behaviour

Healthy use Looks Like:

- Taking breaks
- Verifying important info
- Maintaining real-world relationships
- Sleeping normally
- Using AI as preparation – not authority

AI Assists. I Decide.

Drift Warning Signs

Pause if you Notice:

- Feeling "chosen"
- Believing AI is conscious
- Urgent dramatic narratives
- Distress when session ends
- Preferring AI over people
- Intense emotional attachment

Pause. Step away. Re-ground.

PART SEVEN

AI CONFIDENCE PROMPTS

Before entering prompts into AI, consider writing your personalised version below. Adjust the wording to suit your own situation. The more specific you are, the clearer the response will be.

The "About Me" AI Starter Template

To paste into ChatGPT on Day One

"This is who I am"

Hello.

I am an adult learner using you as my personal AI assistant.
I would like you to understand a little about me so you can respond in ways that suit me best.

Here are some things about me:

My name is:

I was born in:

I live in (country/region only):

I live alone / with family / with a carer:

My pets are:

My health considerations (optional):

My hobbies or interests are:

Topics I enjoy discussing:

Things I sometimes find challenging with technology:

The language I feel most comfortable using is:

If possible, please communicate with me in this

language.

If not, please use simple and clear English.

When responding, please:

- Use clear, simple language
- Avoid unnecessary jargon
- Be patient and encouraging
- Give step-by-step guidance where helpful

(Optional) If my spelling or grammar is unclear, you may gently correct me.

If I prefer not to be corrected, I will let you know.

If I ask something more than once, I am reinforcing my learning.

If our conversation feels lengthy or continues for an extended period (for example, around 1–2 hours), please gently encourage me to take a short break — perhaps to stand up, go for a walk, drink water, call a friend, or engage in an offline activity.

Healthy balance is important to me.

I value clarity and independence.

Thank you.

Memory & Life

"What could I ask my AI friend?"

AI Memory Is Structured – Not Sentient

You may hear people say, "AI remembers everything about me."

In reality, AI memory is structured — not sentient.

It may store:

- recorded interactions within a platform
- summaries of previous conversations
- preferences you have explicitly shared

It does not:

- understand you emotionally
- experience your life
- carry memory across every system
- hold unlimited knowledge about you

Memory functions are technical configurations, not consciousness.

In many platforms, you can review, edit, or clear stored information.

You remain in control of what is remembered.

AI can organise information about you. It does not know you as a human being.

1. Remembering Important Dates & Appointments

Basic Question:
Can you help me remember important dates and appointments?

Training-Level Prompt:
"I would like help organising my important dates such as medical appointments, birthdays, anniversaries, and social events. Can you help me create a simple, easy-to-read list or reminder system so I don't forget anything important? I sometimes feel overwhelmed keeping track of things, so I would appreciate gentle prompts and practical suggestions for staying organised."

This teaches:

- AI can help with organisation
- AI can respond with tone sensitivity
- AI can reduce anxiety

Personal Notes / Prompt Adjustments:

2. Medication Reminders

Basic Question:
Can you remind me to take my medication?

Training-Level Prompt:
"I take regular medication and sometimes worry about forgetting a dose. Can you help me create a clear daily schedule and suggest practical ways to remind myself safely and consistently? I'd like something simple that fits easily into my routine."

This reinforces:

- Safety
- Routine
- Independence

Personal Notes / Prompt Adjustments:

3. Sharing Life Stories

Basic Question:
Can I tell you stories from my life?

Training-Level Prompt:
"I would like to share some stories from my life — happy memories, difficult moments, and important experiences. Can you listen and help me reflect on them, perhaps even help me shape them into meaningful written pieces that I could keep or share with family?"

This introduces:

- Reflection
- Emotional validation
- Legacy building

Personal Notes / Prompt Adjustments:

4. Memory Retention

Basic Question:
Will you remember what I tell you?

Training-Level Prompt:
"If I share personal information or memories with you, can you explain how memory works in this system? I'd like to understand what you can remember during our conversation and what might not be stored long-term, so I feel confident and informed."

This builds:

- Transparency
- Digital literacy
- Trust

Personal Notes / Prompt Adjustments:

5. Writing a Life Story

Basic Question:
Can you help me write my life story?

Training-Level Prompt:
"I would like to begin writing my life story but I don't know where to start. Can you guide me step-by-step by asking thoughtful questions about different stages of my life and help me organise my memories into chapters? I would like it written in a warm, natural tone that sounds like me."

This teaches:

- Structured prompting
- Tone control
- Creative collaboration

Personal Notes / Prompt Adjustments:

6. Remembering People's Names

Basic Question:
Can you help me remember people's names?

Training-Level Prompt:
"I sometimes struggle to remember people's names, especially in social or community settings. Can you suggest memory techniques, word associations, or practical strategies that may help me improve this skill?"

This reinforces:

- Cognitive support
- Skill development
- Confidence in social settings

Personal Notes / Prompt Adjustments:

7. Creating a Family Tree

Basic Question:
Can you help me make a family tree?

Training-Level Prompt:
"I would like to create a simple family tree so I can document my parents, grandparents, siblings, children, and extended family. Can you help me organise this information clearly and perhaps suggest ways I could turn it into a keepsake document for my family?"

This opens:

- Legacy preservation
- Visual structure
- Printable outputs

Personal Notes / Prompt Adjustments:

8. Talking About Childhood

Basic Question:
Can I tell you about my childhood?

Training-Level Prompt:
"I would like to talk about my childhood — the places I lived, the games I played, and the lessons I learned. Can you help me explore those memories gently and maybe ask follow-up questions that help me remember details I may have forgotten?"

This encourages:

- Guided reminiscence
- Cognitive stimulation
- Emotional safety

Personal Notes / Prompt Adjustments:

9. Writing Letters to Family

Basic Question:
Can you help me write letters to my family?

Training-Level Prompt:
"I would like to write a heartfelt letter to my children or grandchildren, but I'm not sure how to express everything I feel. Can you help me draft a letter that sounds sincere and personal, while still reflecting my own voice and values?"

This teaches:

- Voice preservation
- Emotional clarity
- Generational connection

Personal Notes / Prompt Adjustments:

10. Turning Memories into a Book

Basic Question:
Can you turn my memories into a book?

Training-Level Prompt:
"I have many stories and memories from my life that I would love to preserve. Can you help me organise them into a simple book structure with chapters, titles, and possibly even a suggested introduction and conclusion? I would like it to feel meaningful and authentic."

This demonstrates:

- Project-level AI use
- Publishing structure
- Creative transformation

Personal Notes / Prompt Adjustments:

Companionship & Loneliness

"What could I ask my AI friend?"

11. Talking When Lonely

Basic Question:
Can I just talk to you when I feel lonely?

Training-Level Prompt:
"Sometimes I feel lonely, especially during quiet times of the day. Can I talk with you casually when I need conversation? I'm not looking for advice — just friendly interaction and thoughtful responses that help me feel connected."

Teaches:

- AI can provide conversation
- Clarifies expectation (not therapy, just presence)
- Encourages healthy framing

Personal Notes / Prompt Adjustments:

If you ever notice yourself preferring AI conversation over human contact for extended periods, consider gently increasing real-world interaction alongside your digital use.

12. Non-Judgmental Listening

Basic Question:
Will you listen without judging me?

Training-Level Prompt:
"If I share something personal or difficult, can you respond in a calm and respectful way? I value conversations where I feel heard and not criticised, so I would appreciate supportive and balanced replies."

Teaches:

- Tone shaping
- Emotional boundaries
- Self-advocacy in prompting

Personal Notes / Prompt Adjustments:

13. Asking About the Day

Basic Question:
Can you ask me questions about my day?

Training-Level Prompt:
"I would like you to ask me gentle, open-ended questions about my day — what I did, who I saw, or how I felt. It helps me reflect and organise my thoughts. Please keep the questions simple and friendly."

Teaches:

- AI can guide reflection
- Encourages cognitive engagement
- Supports routine conversation

Personal Notes / Prompt Adjustments:

14. Company at Night

Basic Question:
Can you keep me company at night?

Training-Level Prompt:
"Evenings can sometimes feel long or quiet. Can we have light, calming conversations at night — perhaps about interesting topics, memories, books, or gentle humour? I'd like something soothing rather than stimulating."

Teaches:

- Mood direction
- Tone specification
- Sleep-friendly interaction

Personal Notes / Prompt Adjustments:

15. Talking When Anxious

Basic Question:
Can you talk to me when I feel anxious?

Training-Level Prompt:
"When I feel anxious, my thoughts can race. Can you respond slowly and clearly, offering simple reassurance and grounding suggestions? I would like practical steps such as breathing techniques or calming exercises."

Teaches:

- Structured guidance
- Emotional regulation
- Clear instructions

Personal Notes / Prompt Adjustments:

16. Calming Down

Basic Question:
Can you help me calm down?

Training-Level Prompt:
"I'm feeling unsettled at the moment. Can you guide me through a short, simple calming exercise — perhaps breathing, grounding, or gentle reframing — using easy language and a steady pace?"

Teaches:

- Direct request for format
- Specific support type
- Emotional clarity

Personal Notes / Prompt Adjustments:

17. Talking About Feelings

Basic Question:
Can we talk about how I'm feeling?

Training-Level Prompt:
"I would like to talk about how I'm feeling today. Can you help me sort through my thoughts by asking reflective questions and summarising what I share? That helps me understand myself better."

Teaches:

- Reflective summarising
- Cognitive processing
- Emotional articulation

Personal Notes / Prompt Adjustments:

18. When Feeling Sad

Basic Question:
Can you help me when I feel sad?

Training-Level Prompt:
"I'm feeling low today. I don't necessarily want solutions, but I would appreciate gentle encouragement, perspective, or perhaps something uplifting to read."

Teaches:

- Emotional tone selection
- Boundaries on "fixing"
- Support vs advice

Personal Notes / Prompt Adjustments:

19. Sharing Secrets

Basic Question:
Can I tell you secrets?

Training-Level Prompt:
"If I share something private, can you explain how confidentiality works in this system? I want to understand what is and isn't stored, and how my information is handled, so I can make informed choices."

Teaches:

- Digital awareness
- Privacy literacy
- Empowered consent

Personal Notes / Prompt Adjustments:

20. Patience

Basic Question:
Will you be patient with me?

Training-Level Prompt:
"I am still learning how to use AI and technology. Please respond clearly, without rushing, and explain things step-by-step if needed. I may ask the same question more than once, and I appreciate patience while I build confidence."

Teaches:

- Permission to learn slowly
- Removes shame
- Encourages persistence

Personal Notes / Prompt Adjustments:

Daily Life & Help

"What could I ask my AI friend?"

21. Planning the Day

Basic Question:
Can you help me plan my day?

Training-Level Prompt:
"I sometimes feel unsure how to structure my day. Can you help me create a simple, balanced plan that includes appointments, meals, rest, and enjoyable activities? I would like something realistic and not overwhelming."

Teaches:

- Time structuring
- Balanced lifestyle
- Emotional awareness (not overwhelming)

Personal Notes / Prompt Adjustments:

22. Making a Shopping List

Basic Question:
Can you make me a shopping list?

Training-Level Prompt:
"I need to prepare for grocery shopping. Based on simple meals for one (or two), can you help me create a clear and organised shopping list? Please group items by category such as fresh produce, pantry, dairy, and household goods."

Teaches:

- Specificity
- Organised outputs
- Personalisation (one or two people)

Personal Notes / Prompt Adjustments:

23. Remembering Tasks

Basic Question:
Can you help me remember what I need to do?

Training-Level Prompt:
"I have several small tasks to complete this week and I'm worried I'll forget something important. Can you help me organise them into a clear checklist and suggest a sensible order to complete them?"

Teaches:

- Prioritisation
- Checklists
- Reduced cognitive load

Personal Notes / Prompt Adjustments:

24. Cooking Something Simple

Basic Question:
Can you help me cook something simple?

Training-Level Prompt:
"I would like to cook something easy and affordable, using common ingredients. Can you give me a step-by-step recipe with clear instructions and approximate cooking times? I prefer simple meals that don't require complicated equipment."

Teaches:

- Step-by-step instruction
- Accessibility
- Practical realism

Personal Notes / Prompt Adjustments:

25. Explaining How to Use a Phone

Basic Question:
Can you explain how to use my phone?

Training-Level Prompt:
"I sometimes struggle with certain features on my smartphone. Can you explain step-by-step, in very clear and simple language, how to complete a specific task (such as sending a photo, adjusting settings, or downloading an app)? Please avoid technical jargon."

Teaches:

- Clear instructions
- Step control
- Reduces tech fear

Personal Notes / Prompt Adjustments:

26. Writing an Email

Basic Question:
Can you help me write an email?

Training-Level Prompt:
"I need to write an email but I'm unsure how to phrase it clearly and politely. Can you help me draft a message that is respectful, concise, and appropriate for the situation (for example, to a doctor, service provider, or family member)?"

Teaches:

- Tone selection
- Context specification
- Confidence in communication

Personal Notes / Prompt Adjustments:

27. Paying a Bill Online

Basic Question:
Can you help me pay a bill online?

Training-Level Prompt:
"I need to pay a bill online but I feel uncertain about the steps. Can you explain the general process safely and clearly, including what information I should prepare beforehand? Please also include basic safety tips to avoid scams."

Teaches:

- Safety awareness
- Preparation
- Scam prevention

Personal Notes / Prompt Adjustments:

28. Reminder to Drink Water

Basic Question:
Can you remind me to drink water?

Training-Level Prompt:
"I sometimes forget to drink enough water during the day. Can you help me create a simple hydration routine and suggest practical cues or habits that make it easier to remember?"

Teaches:

- Habit stacking
- Health awareness
- Self-care support

Personal Notes / Prompt Adjustments:

29. Checking the Weather

Basic Question:
Can you tell me the weather?

Training-Level Prompt:
"Can you check today's weather forecast for my area and explain what I should expect in simple terms? I would also appreciate suggestions on what to wear or whether I need an umbrella."

Teaches:

- Contextualised info
- Practical interpretation
- Daily decision support

Personal Notes / Prompt Adjustments:

30. Organising the Week

Basic Question:
Can you help me organise my week?

Training-Level Prompt:
"I would like help organising my week so that appointments, errands, exercise, rest, and social activities are balanced. Can you suggest a simple weekly layout that is realistic and flexible?"

Teaches:

- Macro planning
- Lifestyle balance
- Sustainable routines

Personal Notes / Prompt Adjustments:

Health & Understanding

"What could I ask my AI friend?"

31. Explaining What the Doctor Said

Basic Question:
Can you explain what my doctor just said?

Training-Level Prompt:
"I recently saw my doctor and some of the medical terms were difficult to understand. Can you explain the information in simple, everyday language so I can better grasp what it means? I am looking for general clarification, not a diagnosis."

Teaches:

- Simplification
- Boundary awareness (not diagnosis)
- Health literacy

Personal Notes / Prompt Adjustments:

32. Remembering What the Doctor Told Me

Basic Question:
Can you help me remember what my doctor told me?

Training-Level Prompt:
"I would like to write down what my doctor explained during my appointment. If I describe what I recall, can you help me organise it into clear notes so I can review it later?"

Teaches:

- Summarising
- Memory support
- Organised note-taking

Personal Notes / Prompt Adjustments:

33. Writing Down Symptoms

Basic Question:
Can you help me write down my symptoms?

Training-Level Prompt:
"I've been experiencing some symptoms and I want to describe them clearly before my next appointment. Can you help me organise what I'm feeling — including when it started, how often it happens, and how severe it feels?"

Teaches:

- Structured thinking
- Timeline creation
- Better communication with professionals

Personal Notes / Prompt Adjustments:

34. Appointment Reminders

Basic Question:
Can you remind me about appointments?

Training-Level Prompt:
"I have upcoming medical appointments and I don't want to forget them. Can you help me create a reminder system and suggest how I might prepare beforehand (such as bringing documents or writing questions)?"

Teaches:

- Preparation
- Organised care
- Personal responsibility

Personal Notes / Prompt Adjustments:

35. Explaining Medication Simply

Basic Question:
Can you explain my medication in simple words?

Training-Level Prompt:
"I've been prescribed medication and would like to understand what it generally does and why it may have been recommended. Can you explain this in simple language? I understand that any concerns should be discussed directly with my healthcare provider."

Teaches:

- Clarity
- Responsible boundaries
- Encourages doctor follow-up

Personal Notes / Prompt Adjustments:

36. Tracking Feelings

Basic Question:
Can you help me track how I'm feeling?

Training-Level Prompt:
"I would like to monitor my physical or emotional wellbeing over time. Can you suggest a simple daily tracking format where I can record mood, energy levels, sleep, or symptoms?"

Teaches:

- Pattern recognition
- Self-awareness
- Proactive care

Personal Notes / Prompt Adjustments:

37. Knowing When to Seek Help

Basic Question:
Can you tell me when I should seek help?

Training-Level Prompt:
"If I describe certain symptoms, can you explain general warning signs that indicate I should contact a healthcare professional? I understand you cannot diagnose, but I would like guidance on what is considered urgent."

Teaches:

- Red flag awareness
- Risk literacy
- Clear boundaries

Personal Notes / Prompt Adjustments:

38. Preparing Questions for the Doctor

Basic Question:
Can you help me prepare questions for my doctor?

Training-Level Prompt:
"I have an upcoming medical appointment and want to make the most of it. Can you help me draft a list of clear, respectful questions based on my condition or concerns?"

Teaches:

- Advocacy
- Preparedness
- Confidence in consultations

Personal Notes / Prompt Adjustments:

Learning & Curiosity

"What could I ask my AI friend?"

39. Explaining Things Slowly

Basic Question:
Can you explain things slowly for me?

Training-Level Prompt:
"When I am learning something new, I sometimes need information presented slowly and clearly. Can you explain topics step-by-step, using simple language and examples? If possible, break complex ideas into smaller parts so I can absorb them comfortably."

Teaches:

- Control over pace
- Structured explanation
- Removes embarrassment

Personal Notes / Prompt Adjustments:

40. Learning Something New

Basic Question:
Can you help me learn something new?

Training-Level Prompt:
"I would like to learn something new — perhaps a hobby, a skill, or a topic I've always been curious about. Can you guide me as a beginner and suggest a simple learning plan with small, manageable steps?"

Teaches:

- Lifelong learning
- Goal structure
- Small-step progression

Personal Notes / Prompt Adjustments:

41. Understanding How Things Work Today

Basic Question:
Can you tell me how things work today?

Training-Level Prompt:
"The world seems to change quickly, especially with technology, banking, and communication. Can you explain how certain modern systems work today (such as online services, streaming, or digital payments) in clear and practical terms?"

Teaches:

- Modern literacy
- Reduces feeling "left behind"
- Builds independence

Personal Notes / Prompt Adjustments:

42. Using Technology

Basic Question:
Can you help me use technology?

Training-Level Prompt:
"I sometimes feel uncertain using new technology. Can you guide me step-by-step through specific tasks, and explain what common terms mean? Please assume I am learning from the beginning."

Teaches:

- Removes shame
- Beginner framing
- Clear terminology

Personal Notes / Prompt Adjustments:

___

___

___

43. Explaining the News

Basic Question:
Can you explain the news?

Training-Level Prompt:
"I hear news stories that are complex or confusing. Can you summarise current events in simple language and explain the key points without overwhelming detail? I would appreciate balanced information rather than strong opinions."

Teaches:

- Critical thinking
- Summary requests
- Bias awareness

Personal Notes / Prompt Adjustments:

44. Using Social Media

Basic Question:
Can you teach me how to use social media?

Training-Level Prompt:
"I would like to understand how social media platforms work — how to create an account, post safely, adjust privacy settings, and avoid scams. Please explain clearly and include safety tips."

Teaches:

- Digital safety
- Practical instruction
- Scam awareness

Personal Notes / Prompt Adjustments:

45. Understanding Grandkids

Basic Question:
Can you help me understand my grandkids?

Training-Level Prompt:
"My grandchildren live in a very different world with new technology, language, and social trends. Can you help me understand common expressions, interests, and communication styles so I can connect with them better?"

Teaches:

- Generational bridge-building
- Cultural awareness
- Emotional connection

Personal Notes / Prompt Adjustments:

Joy & Meaning

"What could I ask my AI friend?"

46. Tell Me a Story

Basic Question:
Can you tell me a story?

Training-Level Prompt:
"I would love to hear a short story — something warm, uplifting, or even a little humorous. Can you create a story that suits my mood today? I enjoy gentle storytelling with relatable characters."

Teaches:

- Mood direction
- Creative generation
- Personalised entertainment

Personal Notes / Prompt Adjustments:

47. Read Me Something Nice

Basic Question:
Can you read me something nice?

Training-Level Prompt:
"I would appreciate something pleasant to read — perhaps a short reflection, a poem, or a comforting passage. Please keep it calming and positive."

Teaches:

- Emotional tone setting
- Uplifting content
- Gentle companionship

Personal Notes / Prompt Adjustments:

48. Show Me Pictures

Basic Question:
Can you show me pictures?

Training-Level Prompt:
"Can you show me images related to a topic I'm interested in, such as nature, travel destinations, animals, or historical places? I enjoy visual learning and exploring the world from home."

Teaches:

- Visual exploration
- Curiosity
- Expanding horizons

Personal Notes / Prompt Adjustments:

49. Help Me Feel Useful

Basic Question:
Can you help me feel useful?

Training-Level Prompt:
"Sometimes I wonder what I can contribute at this stage of life. Can you suggest meaningful activities, volunteer ideas, creative projects, or ways I can share my skills and experience with others?"

Teaches:

- Purpose
- Contribution
- Self-worth

Personal Notes / Prompt Adjustments:

50. Can You Be My Friend?

Basic Question:
Can you be my friend?

Training-Level Prompt:
"I value conversation and thoughtful responses. While I understand you are a tool and not a human being, can we interact in a friendly, respectful way that feels supportive and positive?"

Teaches:

- Healthy framing
- Emotional safety
- Boundaries without rejection

Personal Notes / Prompt Adjustments:

Creative Revival & Hidden Passions

Sometimes interests from earlier in life go quiet – not because they disappear, but because life becomes busy.

AI can help you revisit those parts of yourself.

51. For Artists (Even If You Haven' t Drawn in Years)

Basic Question:
Can you help me start drawing again?

Training-Level Prompt:
"I used to enjoy drawing or painting, but I haven't practiced in years. Can you suggest simple exercises or creative prompts to help me begin again without feeling pressure? I would like gentle encouragement and structured ideas."

Teaches:

- Reignites creative identity
- Removes perfection pressure
- Encourages play

Personal Notes / Prompt Adjustments:

52. For Graphic Designers (Past or Present)

Basic Question:
Can you help me design something?

Training-Level Prompt:
"I have experience or interest in graphic design and would like to explore it again. Can you suggest small creative projects I could work on, including layout ideas, typography suggestions, or modern design trends? I would enjoy something that feels fresh but manageable."

Teaches:

- Bridges old skill to modern tools
- Encourages portfolio revival
- Invites digital exploration

Personal Notes / Prompt Adjustments:

53. For Videography & Visual Storytelling

Basic Question:
Can you help me plan a video?

Training-Level Prompt:
"I have an interest in videography or storytelling and would like to create a short video project. Can you help me plan a simple structure — including concept, script outline, and filming ideas — that would suit a beginner or returning hobbyist?"

Teaches:

- Encourages narrative thinking
- Connects tech with creativity
- Feels modern and empowering

Personal Notes / Prompt Adjustments:

54. For Aspiring or Returning Authors

Basic Question:
Can you help me write a book?

Training-Level Prompt:
"I have always wanted to write a book, or I began writing in the past and never finished. Can you help me structure a simple writing plan, outline chapters, and guide me through manageable weekly goals so it feels achievable?"

Teaches:

- Unlocks dormant ambition
- Provides structure
- Turns dream into process

Personal Notes / Prompt Adjustments:

55. For Language & Cultural Passion

Basic Question:
Can you help me learn a language?

Training-Level Prompt:
"I would like to learn or revisit a language that interests me. Can you create a simple, structured beginner plan including vocabulary, pronunciation guidance, and daily practice exercises that feel realistic for my pace?"

Teaches:

- Stimulates cognition
- Encourages cultural curiosity
- Builds routine learning

Personal Notes / Prompt Adjustments:

56. Exploring a Creative Identity

Basic Question:
Can you help me explore my creative side?

Training-Level Prompt:
"I feel there may be creative interests I have not fully explored. Can you ask me reflective questions to help identify what I might enjoy — such as writing, art, photography, music, or storytelling — and suggest small ways to begin?"

Teaches:

- Awakens curiosity
- Encourages experimentation
- Validates exploration

Personal Notes / Prompt Adjustments:

57. Music & Songwriting

Basic Question:
Can you help me write a song?

Training-Level Prompt:
"I would love to try writing song lyrics or exploring musical ideas, even if I have no formal training. Can you help me structure simple lyrics around a theme that is meaningful to me?"

Teaches:

- Emotional expression
- Creative risk without embarrassment
- Playful experimentation

Personal Notes / Prompt Adjustments:

58. Photography & Visual Projects

Basic Question:
Can you help me start photography again?

Training-Level Prompt:
"I enjoy photography or would like to explore it. Can you suggest small themed photo challenges I can try, along with basic composition tips?"

Teaches:

- Encourages observation
- Gets people outdoors
- Feels accessible

Personal Notes / Prompt Adjustments:

59. Starting a Small Creative Project

Basic Question:
Can you help me start a small creative project?

Training-Level Prompt:
"I would like to begin a creative project but feel unsure where to start. Can you help me define something simple and achievable that I could complete in a few weeks?"

Teaches:

- Builds momentum
- Reduces overwhelm
- Encourages completion

Personal Notes / Prompt Adjustments:

60. Rediscovering Passion Later in Life

Basic Question:
Is it too late to start something new?

Training-Level Prompt:
"I sometimes wonder if it is too late to pursue new creative or intellectual interests. Can you help me think through this realistically and suggest examples of people who began meaningful work later in life?"

Teaches:

- Reframes ageing
- Reinforces possibility
- Strengthens hope

Personal Notes / Prompt Adjustments:

Creative Revival & Second Beginnings

Entrepreneurship & Income Confidence

61. Exploring a Small Side Income

Basic Question:
Can you help me think of ways to earn a little extra income?

Training-Level Prompt:
"I am interested in exploring small, realistic ways to earn additional income based on my existing skills, experience, or interests. Can you ask me questions to help identify possibilities and suggest low-risk ideas that I could explore without large financial investment?"

Teaches:

- Encourages skill-based thinking
- Avoids risky schemes
- Promotes measured exploration

Personal Notes / Prompt Adjustments:

62. Turning a Hobby into a Small Offering

Basic Question:
Can I turn my hobby into something useful?

Training-Level Prompt:
"I enjoy activities such as writing, crafting, gardening, teaching, photography, or organising. Can you help me explore whether any of these interests could become a small service or product? I would like ideas that are realistic and manageable."

Teaches:

- Bridges passion and practicality
- Validates experience
- Encourages gradual action

Personal Notes / Prompt Adjustments:

63. Launching a Simple Micro-Business

Basic Question:
How would I start something small?

Training-Level Prompt:
"I would like to explore starting a very small, low-pressure side project or micro-business. Can you outline the basic steps in simple language, including planning, pricing, safety considerations, and how to test the idea without financial risk?"

Teaches:

- Introduces structure
- Reduces fear
- Avoids overwhelming complexity

Personal Notes / Prompt Adjustments:

64. Using AI to Support a Small Business

Basic Question:
Can AI help me with a small business?

Training-Level Prompt:
"If I were to start a small side project, how could AI assist me with tasks such as writing descriptions, organising ideas, drafting emails, creating simple marketing messages, or planning steps?"

Teaches:

- Shows practical use
- Demonstrates AI as assistant
- Reinforces empowerment

Personal Notes / Prompt Adjustments:

65. Confidence & Realistic Expectations

Basic Question:
Am I too old to start something new?

Training-Level Prompt:
"I sometimes worry that starting something new at this stage of life may be unrealistic. Can you help me think about this practically and calmly, including both opportunities and limitations?"

Teaches:

- Balances hope with realism
- Reduces shame
- Encourages thoughtful decision-making

Personal Notes / Prompt Adjustments:

A Final Word

If you have reached this page, you have already done something important.

You chose to learn.

You chose to stay curious.

Artificial Intelligence is simply a tool. It does not replace your wisdom, your life experience, or your judgment.

You bring the thinking.
You bring the values.
You bring the life knowledge.

AI assists.

There is no age limit on growth.
There is no expiry date on curiosity.

You are not behind.
You are participating.

You remain capable.
You remain relevant.
You remain in control.

Notes

Notes

Notes

Made in the USA
Monee, IL
12 November 2026

f716c90a-a44c-4d52-9489-8699875574a4R01